KING ABDULAZIZ... HIS PLANE AND HIS PILOT

Michael Saba PhD

GulfAmerica Press

SPECIAL COLLECTORS EDITION

Copyright 2009

Published by GulfAmerica Press
PO Box 32
Sioux Falls, SD 57101-0032

ISBN 978-1-61584-082-3
Library of Congress 2009906314

We would like to thank the Custodian of the Two Holy Mosques for his support of this project.

The Custodian of the Two Holy Mosques, King Abdullah bin Abdulaziz Al Saud; Joe Grant, 101 years of age and Dr. Michael Saba, the author.

We would also like to thank HRH Crown Prince Sultan bin Abdulaziz Al Saud, First Deputy Premier and Minister of Defense and Aviation and Inspector General for his assistance in making this project a reality.

HRH Crown Prince Sultan bin Abdulaziz Al Saud.

Acknowledgements

In the presentation of this book there have been many people and organizations who have given much of their time and their resources and we would like to sincerely acknowledge that support and to thank them.

HRH Prince Sultan bin Salman bin Abdulaziz Al Saud

HRH has facilitated this project using his energy and abilities in bringing everyone together personally and arranging meetings with HM, the King and other senior Royal Family members. Without him this book would never have been produced.

Al Turath Foundation

The Al Turath Foundation has provided sponsorship and assistance in accessing archives and information and has made this project a reality. Special thanks to Dr. Zahir Othman.

Boeing

The story of civil aviation in the Kingdom began with the DC-3 produced by the Douglas Corporation. Over the years as companies grow and develop this legacy has ended up under the care of the Boeing Corporation. From the first approaches Boeing was helpful and supportive in providing access to their archives and the archives of the Douglas Corporation in California. We would like to mention a few names of people at Boeing who gave of their time and energy.

>Shep Hil, Charlie Miller, Ahmed Al Jazzar, Omar Shesha, Mary Kane, Capt. Stephen Taylor and Robert Johnstone

Joe Grant

Joe Grant and his wife Marga have given much to the telling of this story; Joe has held a lifelong love of the Kingdom which was reaffirmed in 2006 when he and Marga traveled back at the invitation of HRH Salman bin Abdulaziz. Joe's energy and enthusiasm for everything he does is an inspiration to all who meet him. A significant portion of the photographs were published from Joe Grant's personal collection.

King Abdulaziz Foundation for Research and Archives

We would like to recognize and thank the King Abdulaziz Foundation for Research and Archives, Dr. Fahd Al Semmari, and the foundation's staff for the access to their archives and for the time and attention they set aside.

Saudi Arabian Airlines

We would like to recognize and thank Saudi Arabian Airlines for the materials and information they provided.

Saudi Aramco

We would like to recognize and thank Saudi Aramco and their staff for the access to their archives and for the time and attention they set aside and the subsequent delivery of photographs and artifacts.

Royal Aviation

We would like to recognize and thank Mr. Bob Reid of Royal Aviation who under Boeing assisted in the restoration of SA-R-1 to flying condition. They supplied photographs of the restoration.

Al Jazeerah Aviation Museum

We would like to recognize and thank the management and staff of Al Jazeerah Aviation Museum for allowing photographs of SA-R-1 and the museum.

We would like to recognize and thank the Production Crew:

Doug Anderson, Bruce Wendt, Joe Knue, Irene Hansen, Tom Block, Linda Block

Saudi Research and Marketing

We would like to thank Saudi Research and Marketing for assisting in the production of this book.

We would also like to thank:

Edward Grant, Tacey Grant, Marga Grant
Jim Bleth, Khalid Nasser, Roger Harrison, Dr. Selwa Al Hazza, Ken Hoffman,
Hassan Husseini, Daniel Saba, and the many others who made this project a reality.

Appreciations

Khalid Al Melhem, Director General of Saudi Araian Airlines...

As Director General of the largest airline in the Middle East and the 25th largest in the world, I would like to thank Captain Joe Grant for his role in helping to create Saudi Arabian Airlines. From the first airplane in our fleet, the DC-3 that Captain Joe flew into Saudi Arabia in 1945, to today, Saudi Arabian Airlines has made an indelible mark on the world airline scene.

Ahmed Al Jazzar, President of Boeing, Saudi Arabia...

Boeing is proud to be part of the legacy of aviation in Saudi Arabia. This legacy began when Captain Joe Grant flew a DC-3, the gift of then, President Franklin Delano Roosevelt to King Abdulaziz in 1945. Captain Joe Grant will forever remain part of this great Saudi aviation history.

Dedicated to:
Marga "Schatzi" Wipperfeld Grant
February 27, 1924-August 25, 2008

"We Love You More."

Contents

Foreword..................................10
Introduction..............................11
King Abdulaziz Ibn Saud...................14
Early February, 1945......................19
Promise of Oil............................44
Artifacts.................................73
Restoration...............................84
June 2009 Visit..........................101
Epilogue.................................106
Postscript...............................108
About the Author.........................109
Credits..................................111

Foreword

When visitors come to Saudi Arabia, and they disembark into the vast halls of the airports at Riyadh, or Jeddah or any of the many airports in the Kingdom, they often talk about the changes that have taken place in the Kingdom in so few years. They are talking about large modern cities, highways, and so on. But when I'm asked about what I see as the biggest changes that have take place here, sometimes what I think about is time. I think that the modern world has changed the way we measure and experience time.

Think about this. When my Grandfather, King Abdulaziz united the regions of this peninsula into the Kingdom of Saudi Arabia in 1932, travel and movement for people here was much the same as it had been for millennia—measured in days and even months. In a land where there were no roads, where the sand shifted with the desert winds, that was one of the hard realities of life. I think it's safe to say that no one, here or perhaps anywhere, could have imagined that in just over 50 years, I myself would be circling the entire globe in an hour and a half.

It's not space travel, though, that began the change. In Saudi Arabia it was the airplane. The modern world came to Saudi Arabia on metal wings, with two roaring engines. The year was 1945, and the airplane was a DC-3.

This book is a look at the development of civil aviation in Saudi Arabia and some of the changes to the Kingdom that have taken place assisted by the development of the ability to fly around the Kingdom. Creating the book came about because of some wonderful experiences. A few years ago, people in the Kingdom and people in the United States wanted to commemorate a historic meeting between King Abdulaziz and then-President Franklin Roosevelt. In the course of planning that event, there was a great deal of talk about the DC-3 airplane which was presented to my grandfather by the President. Later, we found that a man who had been assigned to fly that airplane for the King was still living, a former TWA Captain named Joe Grant. Not only was Joe Grant still living, but he had a wealth of stories about flying in the Kingdom in those days, about how commercial aviation got started in the kingdom, and what it was like for him to live in Saudi Arabia before the modern world took hold. Joe Grant has turned 101 years old in 2009, and is still going strong.

In a nutshell, that's what this pictorial history is about: the King, airplanes, people, and change. It's interesting, now, to think about aviation and the future in Saudi Arabia. What changes can it bring about? Not long ago, I saw Saudi Arabia from the perspective of a glider pilot: mountains, volcanoes, and sweeping dunes. I saw my country perhaps as birds see it, in the way that they have seen it for millennia. Maybe now, instead of pushing us faster into the modern world, aviation can take us back, can remind us of where we live, the place and the people we come from.

HRH Sultan bin Salman bin Abdulaziz Al Saud
President- Al Turath Foundation
Chairman-Founder-The Saudi Aviation Club

Introduction

With this brief history, we hope to present a snapshot of the development of aviation in the Kingdom of Saudi Arabia. Although the project is by no means an exhaustive or technical study, it captures the spirit of the pioneers of a most technical industry in what was, in the 1940's, a new desert nation. The project evolved over several years after, almost by accident, I met a most amazing man who played a unique role in early Saudi aviation: Joe Grant. When I met Joe, he was ninety-eight years old. As a young WW II veteran, Joe was one of the first to fly in the Kingdom, becoming the pilot of King Abdulaziz Al Saud, the founder and first king of Saudi Arabia. This project is the King's story, it is Joe's story, and it is a small chapter in the history of aviation.

This pictorial retrospective would not have been possible without the support, assistance, and inspiration of the Boeing Companies, headquartered in the United States, and the Al Turath Foundation of Saudi Arabia. In 1998, Boeing, which now is almost synonymous with "airplane," commemorated what was then a fifty-five year old aviation relationship with the Kingdom of Saudi Arabia with a project to restore the original DC-3 that was King Abdulaziz's first airplane. The DC-3 was a gift to the King from President Franklin Roosevelt; it was flown across the Kingdom by Joe Grant. This project celebrates that gift and the ongoing relationship between the United States and Saudi Arabia.

The Boeing Companies in Saudi Arabia

Five of the pioneer giants of civil aviation- The Boeing Aircraft Company, and Douglas Aircraft Company, The McDonnell Aircraft Corporation, North American Aviation, and Hughes Aircraft-comprise today's Boeing Companies. Most of these companies, or the men that founded them, played a role in the development of aviation in the Kingdom of Saudi Arabia as well as in the United States. They are now part of Boeing's history as well.

Boeing's relationship with Saudi Arabia can be traced back to the early days of Douglas Aircraft. Donald Douglas incorporated the Douglas Aircraft Company in 1921. The first major project of the fledgling company was to design and build an airplane capable of flying around the world. The Douglas World Cruiser was based on the earlier Douglas design of a Navy Torpedo bomber, the DT-2. Douglas Aircraft constructed five World Cruisers, four for the actual attempt to fly around the world and one for testing and training exercises. The four "expedition" airplanes left Seattle on April 4, 1924. Two completed the trip, returning to Seattle on September 28, 1924-175 days, or approximately 371 flying hours-after departing. Coincidently one of the pilots that completed this journey was Leigh Wade, Joe grant's uncle. Joe learned to fly from his uncle Leigh Wade. These around-the-world flights established the Douglas Aircraft Corporation as a major player in the aviation world. Douglas Aircraft has been part of the Boeing Companies since 1997, when Boeing merged with McDonnell Douglas.

Douglas Aircraft

Like most of the first aerospace companies, Douglas Aircraft depended on the military to stay aloft in the years after World War I. Most of its designs were based on the DT and World Cruiser, and were used by the military as observation planes, transports, and to carry mail. By the late 1920's, however, aircraft designers were moving beyond biplanes like the DT design and began to compete to make commercial air travel a profitable business. When Boeing built the Model 247, it appeared that the competition might come to an abrupt end. But Boeing was committed to building aircraft for its own airlines, United Airlines. When Howard Hughes, the owner of TWA, could not persuade Boeing to sell him the Model 247, he requested bids for another transport. Donald Douglas won the bid with the design of the DC-I, which was both larger and faster than the 247. The production version of the DC-I, the DC-2, went into service in 1934, and airlines lined-up to buy the new airliner. American Airlines responded to the competition with the concept of a "sleeper" service for cross county flights. Douglas Aircraft designed the DC-3, a larger version of the DC-2, that could be set up for 14 passengers with sleeping berths or for 21 passengers for "daytime" travel. The DC-3 went into service in 1935 and became the standard against which other aircraft were measured. A new era in commercial aviation had dawned.

In 1945, Franklin D. Roosevelt gave King Abdulaziz of Saudi Arabia a DC-3 to commemorate their meeting on board the USS Quincy on February 14 of that year (see pages 19-28 of this book). The airplane, registered as SA-R-1, became the first of three "royal" DC-3's, and later an airliner in the growing fleet of Saudi Arabian Airlines. (For more of the history of SA-R-1 and its Boeing-sponsored restoration, see pages 84-91 of this book.) Douglas Aircraft continued its relationship with Saudi Arabian Airlines with each of its new generation of aircraft-the DC-4, the DC-6, and in the jet age the DC-8 and DC-9. Douglas Aircraft merged with the McDonnell Aircraft Corporation in 1967 and, as noted, became part of the Boeing Companies in 1997.

North American Aviation

North American Aviation began to manufacture airplanes in 1934, under the direction of former Douglas Aircraft engineers and designers. Like Douglas and other aviation companies, its primary client was the military, but, rather than compete head-to-head with Douglas and Boeing the manufacture of large, multi-engine aircraft, North American Aviation directed its efforts at small, single-engine trainers and observation planes. In the years before World War II, its primary production aircraft was the BT-9-the "Basic Trainer." As the need for trained pilots exploded during World War II, the manufacture of trainers went into high gear, and so did the manufacture of bombers and fighter aircraft. North American Aviation produced 41,000 airplanes during the war years, including B-25 bombers. AT-6 trainers, and P-51 Mustang fighters. After the war, the AT-6 became the T-6, which remains a popular trainer.

After the war, the company had to retool for a new era of aircraft. It shifted production to commercial aircraft with the Navion, and in the jet-age with the B-45 Tornado. It was with the T-6 and the Navion that North American Aviation found a niche in the civil aviation program in the Kingdom of Saudi Arabia.

In 1946, Transcontinental and Western Airlines (TWA) entered into an agreement with Saudi Arabia to assist the Kingdom to develop a domestic airline and to train Saudis in all phases of operation, from flying to administration. In 1952, the Kingdom entered into an agreement with the United States to assist in the development of the Royal Saudi Air Force. In addition to the DC-3's (and its military counterpart, the C-47), T-6 trainers and Harvards (a British/Canadian version of the T-6), were used to train Saudi civilian and military pilots. (See page 66 of this book). True to North American Aviation roots, the Navion found a unique niche in the Kingdom, becoming an essential tool for the Arab American Oil Company (Aramco, now Saudi Aramco).

These small, single-engine four-passenger aircraft were ideal for use in the desert in locations where larger aircraft that needed far longer landing strips and refueling stations were unsuitable. (See pages 45 and 46 of this book.) In the 1950's and 1960's, North American Aviation entered the jet-age with military fighters and bombers. Some of these aircraft, such as the F-86 Sabre, became part of the Royal Saudi Air Force arsenal. Today, some of these aircraft are displayed at the Saqr Al Jazeerah Air Museum in Riyadh. (See pages 95 and 96 of this book). In 1967, North American merged with the Rockwell Standard Corporation to venture into space flight; the combined companies joined the Boeing family in 1996.

Howard Hughes

It is difficult to overstate the influence of Howard Hughes on early aviation in the United States, and his influence on the development of aviation in Saudi Arabia is equally profound. Howard Hughes owned TWA, which in 1946 negotiated two agreements with the Kingdom. One agreement allowed the airline to begin commercial service from the U.S. to Dhahran, Saudi Arabia, as a stop on a route to Bombay, India. The other gave TWA a role in assisting the Kingdom to develop its domestic airline. The relationship between TWA and what became the Saudi Arabian Airlines lasted for 30 years. TWA Captain Joe Grant served as the personal pilot of King Abdulaziz and the royal family from 1945-47. Joe eventually retired from TWA in 1967. Joe Grant traversed the airspace of Saudi Arabia in SA-R-1 and other "royal" DC-3's. (See pages 29-42 of this book).

Howard Hughes became interested in aviation as a pilot, setting speed records for trans-continental and around-the-world flights. His first records were set in aircraft designed by his own company, the Hughes Aircraft Development Group (part of Hughes Tool Company). In 1936, the Development Group became the Hughes Aircraft Company. Most famous for building the Spruce Goose, a huge transport constructed primarily of wood, the Hughes Aircraft Company survived the war years by building aircraft sub-assemblies for other aircraft companies. After the war, Hughes' manufacturing interests took other directions, with the aircraft division developing helicopters. Another offshoot, the Hughes Electronics Corporation, concentrated on missiles and electronics. Hughes Space & Communications, a subsidiary of Hughes Electronics, developed satellite systems and other space communications. Howard Hughes died in 1976, but his influence lives on.

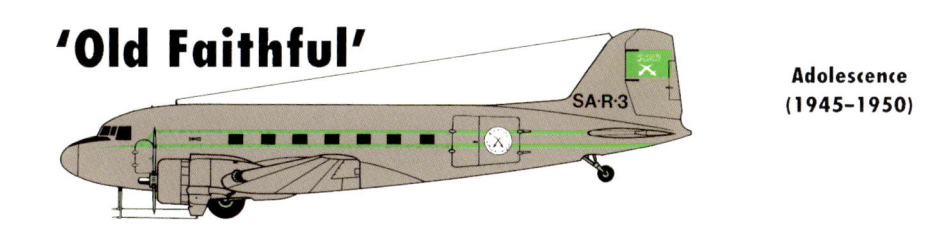

'Old Faithful'

SA-R-3

Adolescence
(1945-1950)

King Abdulaziz Ibn Saud

The man who united the regions of the Arabian Peninsula, was among the great men of our age. Today King Abdulaziz is most often seen in images from a time well past his youth—seated discussing the affairs of the world with other leaders, Franklin Roosevelt, or Winston Churchill. But other images (**right**, *by Captain William Shakespear, taken in 1910*) may display more of the man who left his home-in-exile in Kuwait, 1901, with sixty-three men and a fierce ambition—to retake the lands ruled by his ancestors a hundred years before. "His natural endowments of exceptional astuteness and judgment of men, along with an indomitable will…enabled him to weld together in half a century the warring tribes of the Arabian desert into the kingdom which bore his name."

But the Arabia that became his kingdom in 1932 bore no resemblance to the Kingdom of Saudi Arabia of today. No one could have imagined the glass and concrete cities of Jeddah and Riyadh in the adobe-walled villages of that time. It may be that the best way to illuminate how it could have taken place is to see the emergence of the kingdom in the context of its historical moment.

As a Kingdom, Saudi Arabia stepped onto the world stage just as (for example) oil became a sought-after resource. It emerged just as the Douglas Aircraft Company brought out an aircraft that would prove to make air travel accessible to ordinary people (and at the same time a profitable venture for airlines). Thus Saudi Arabia was founded as technology and science were shrinking distances, and reshaping the world in terms of wealth and power.

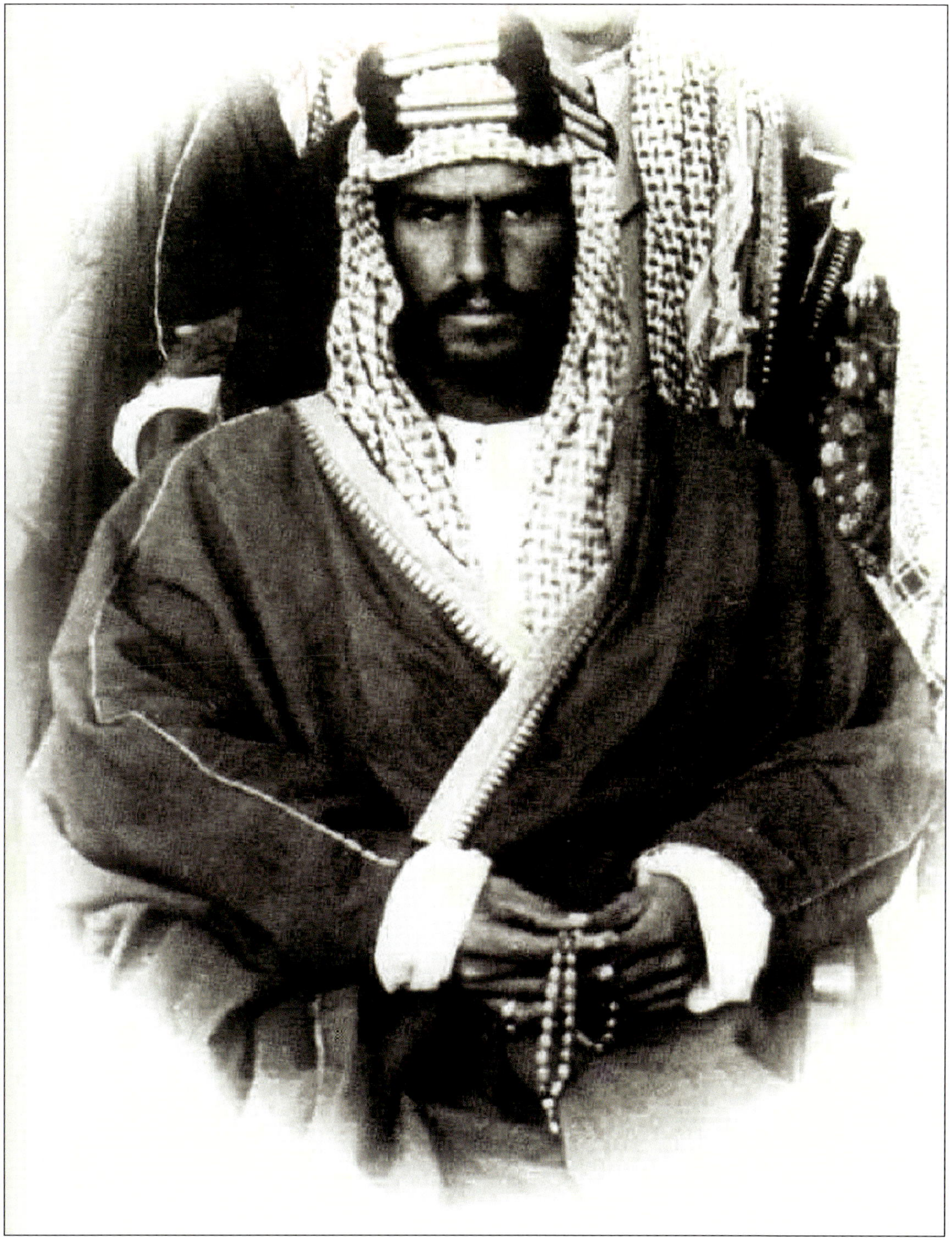

KING ABDULAZIZ, HIS PLANE AND HIS PILOT

It is well outside the scope of this little history to elaborate on how King Abdulaziz united his kingdom by means of conquest and a shrewd understanding of the loyalties at work in the regions of his birth. In any case it is hard to imagine that the weapons available to him, and an intimate knowledge of tribal culture would have placed him, a dozen years hence, discussing the shape of the post-war world with FDR and Winston Churchill. There is more at work here.

It's a truism to say that in most cases it would have been impossible to predict historical events by the decisions and actions that set them in motion. In 1932, the loyalty of parts of Abdulaziz's nascent kingdom could hardly have been taken for granted. By means of power and skillful diplomacy, the King had allied some tribes to himself, but much of his support was based on his personality and qualities. In the midst of world-wide depression, revenue had dwindled. It is no coincidence that within a year, the kingdom had signed an oil concession with the company that became the Arabian American Oil Company.

It was, without doubt, a pragmatic decision like other pragmatic decisions the King had made as he united and consolidated his kingdom. Fate had placed oil under his feet, and that oil would help him fulfill his ambition. It is not hard to follow the thread from this decision to the King's meeting with Franklin Roosevelt on board the USS Quincy in 1945, and from that to an airplane, from an airplane to a pilot, and finally to the infancy of civil aviation in Saudi Arabia.

(*left*, *a portrait of King Abdulaziz Ibn Saud circa:1950*)

King Abdulaziz, his plane and his pilot

HM King Abdulaziz meets Franklin Delano Roosevelt with Colnel William A. Eddy, aboard the USS Quincy, February 14, 1945.

Early February, 1945

Franklin Delano Roosevelt, President of the United States, Winston Churchill, Prime Minister of Great Britain, and Joseph Stalin, Premier of the Union of Soviet Socialist Republics, met at Yalta to negotiate the shape of the post-war world. Each was attempting to shape the future to their national interests. As he returned from this conference, Franklin Delano Roosevelt asked to meet with other men, leaders, who, in his vision, held resources that would be important in the coming years. First among them was King Abdulaziz, on February 14th.

Their meeting was brief, some five or six hours of conversation. No written complete transcript of all that the two men talked about is available yet. But by all accounts, they found in each other congenial company, a kind of like-mindedness—as King Abdulaziz is reported to have said, they had much in common, being both heads of state with grave responsibilities who "bore in their bodies grave physical infirmities."

During their meeting, the President gave the King his spare wheelchair. But Roosevelt wanted to give King Abdulaziz a greater gift, to acknowledge their personal friendship and the link between the two nations. The gift took the form of an airplane, the venerable DC-3.

The gift DC-3 arrived in the Kingdom of Saudi Arabia on April 14, 1945, just two days following Franklin Roosevelt's death, and just over a week since the final correspondence between the two leaders. Colonel William A. Eddy, who was the American minister in Saudi Arabia, and who had interpreted for the King and the President aboard the Quincy, formally presented the airplane to Prince Mansur, who was the son of King Abdulaziz and also the Defense Minister of Saudi Arabia. Each gave a speech about the airplane and the relationship between the two nations.

Mansur spoke for the Kingdom: "In the name of my father, His Majesty Abdulaziz Ibn Saud, I accept gratefully this most handsome airplane, a gift from his beloved friend, President Roosevelt. The Kingdom of Saudi Arabia will value this gift for many reasons in addition to its valuable service in transportation: it will always recall the giver, your late President, for whom His Majesty conceived unparalleled admiration; it will knit more firmly the strands of friendship between our nations as it weaves its way back and forth over our land, guided by American hands…

SAR 1 President Roosevelt's gift to Saudi Arabia. This picture and the following pages are from Joe Grant's personal collection, the King Abdulaziz Foundation and the Al Turath Foundation.

There had been airplanes in the Kingdom before. During the First World War, Britain's Royal Flying Corps, No. 14 Squadron, had operated in the Hejaz region. In 1925, after the war, Sharif Hussein Ibn Ali, the ruler of the Hejaz at that time, acquired six De Havilland 9 combat aircraft from Germany. These aircraft were eventually used to attack Abdulaziz's positions, even flying missions over Makkah in December. When Sharif Ali finally surrendered to Abdulaziz in December, the future King of Saudi Arabia, acquired these airplanes as spoils of war.

The experience of being bombed evidently persuaded Abdulaziz of the value of airplanes for military purposes. From December, 1925 until the Second World War, King Abdulaziz slowly built the basis for a Royal Saudi Air Force, buying military aircraft and building airfields at Jeddah and Taif. These were of British and European manufacture—Wapitis, Italian Capronis, and French Caudrons. Saudi pilots were sent to Italy and later to Cairo for training.

(Above) King Abdulaziz at the Jeddah airfield in 1928. The aircraft may be one of the captured DH 9s.

(Left) King Abdulaziz inspecting one of the Capronis in 1936.

KING ABDULAZIZ, HIS PLANE AND HIS PILOT

The DC-3 was a different breed of airplane. Developed to fly passengers in unprecedented comfort and style, the DC-3 also had speed and range—in short, it was big, it was fast, and perhaps most importantly, it was modern. Like his stately Pierce-Arrow car, the DC-3 was an airplane worthy of a king.

Even more, the DC-3 was symbolic of the King's ascendance into the modern world. "With the advent of the DC-3, the airframe revolution was complete and the modern airliner had arrived. ….The aircraft established a standard against which other airliners were measured." Certainly no other aircraft of the era could have created such a stir.

KING ABDULAZIZ, HIS PLANE AND HIS PILOT

27

King Abdulaziz, his plane and his pilot

There is little record of King Abdulaziz himself actually flying in the airplane for the first months following its delivery. When the airplane was delivered, the arrangement was for American army pilots to fly it, rotated every couple of months.

Records show that the airplane was used to fly members of the American legation in Saudi Arabia, and military personnel. On August 8, 1945, William Eddy, then the American minister in Jeddah, wrote to the Secretary of State "…Lieut. Colonels Shumate and Ellis and a Captain of the A.T.C. flew from Cairo to Jidda ….Stormy weather, however, prevented the plane from landing at Jidda and they spent the night at Port Sudan where their plane landed only with the greatest difficulty. They arrived at Jidda the next day, only two hours before the arrival of General Giles with Shaikh Yusuf Yassin….On August 5, the entire party proceeded to Riyadh on the King's plane, returning to Jidda August 8." Records show that the King first flew in his gift airplane on September 30, 1945, flying from Afif to Taif.

After the war's end, the arrangements for military pilots continued for a time, but because of a lack of suitable housing for the pilots in Jeddah, the military recommended that the plane and crews be moved to Cairo, "even though their withdrawal means that the king's plane will be inoperative for some time to come."

Thus the value of the airplane to King Abdulaziz might have remained largely symbolic. It appears, however, that early in 1946 negotiations were carried out with TWA (then Transcontinental and Western Airlines) to turn over the job of flying the plane to civilian pilots.

King Abdulaziz, his plane and his pilot

The man who got the job of King's pilot was Joe Grant, and he would stay with the King and the airplane for two years.

As much as the DC-3 was the right airplane for King Abdulaziz's vision for the Kingdom, it needed the right pilot. The King needed a pilot who could take him anyplace, who would look at the kind of flying he was going to have to do and think, as Joe Grant says himself, it was fun. When King Abdulaziz got Joe Grant, he got the right man for the job.

Joe says that flying the King was like "the old barnstorming days," going places where there weren't any landing strips much less any of the navigational aids of the time. Sometimes he didn't know where they were going, but the desert people did, and that was all right with Joe. For Joe Grant, flying the King was his job. "The King, he was the man I was working for." "We could take him anyplace in that desert." And he came to admire the people and the culture, so that when he finally left the Kingdom, he had become part of it. It was a part of him.

KING ABDULAZIZ, HIS PLANE AND HIS PILOT

"Most of our co-pilots were Saudis—we had four of them—Hamza Terrabzoni I liked best, and usually when I flew the King I would get Hamza."
   Joe Grant

33

KING ABDULAZIZ, HIS PLANE AND HIS PILOT

"You'd see a cloud of dust coming across the desert, one guard on each side on the running board—what an experience! Something to see..."   *Joe Grant*

KING ABDULAZIZ, HIS PLANE AND HIS PILOT

As early as 1926, King Abdulaziz had thought of using his captured military aircraft for mail and commercial traffic. But the first real push to establish a domestic airline the Kingdom came during the war years and immediately after, as TWA entered into negotiations with the Kingdom. In September, 1946, the Kingdom signed an agreement with TWA to develop the airline. Joe Grant and another TWA pilot and mechanic, Mark Outhwaite, flew to Cairo to buy additional surplus C-47s. According to Joe, they bought five, and had three of them converted to passenger use. Thus, by February 1947 the Kingdom had six DC-3s flying, three with the "royal" registration SA-R, and the others with a new SA-A registration. One record indicates that there were ten DC-3s flying by August, 1947.

The agreement was for TWA to operate and manage the airline for five years—a relationship that turned out to be much longer. The vision of the King was that with domestic airline service, the far-flung regions of the kingdom would be drawn closer, if not in distance, certainly in time. And international service, especially in the region, would make the pilgrimage to Makkah more feasible. But it would take a few more years for infrastructure to catch up with the vision.

A slide showing a runway in the desert.

KING ABDULAZIZ, HIS PLANE AND HIS PILOT

" We were an airline without airports"
Joe Grant

" As we began to collect the money for ticket sales, I kept it in a footlocker at the foot of my bed, I had to call the minister of finance to find out what to do with it."   Joe Grant

Joe Grant spent two years in Saudi Arabia, mostly flying the King and the royal family. As his time wore on, he saw other pilots in Cairo and Beirut flying new aircraft, and he began to feel left behind. He tells the story like this...

> *They were getting more airplanes, and all I was doing was sitting back there in a DC-3. And that bugged me. I thought I was missing out on some of the fun. And I was.... But what did they put me in when I got back here [to] TWA? They put me flying DC-3s. I'll tell you, when I first got ... there in Kansas City, and they put me back in school and said hey, you've got to get modernized, and they beat me down a bit, and I felt like, "What in the world are you doing here? What did I ever leave Saudi Arabia for?" I would have swum back, almost, to get back there. Because there I was happy. I was happy in Saudi Arabia. Probably it was all the challenges...*

There were plenty of those, even for an old barnstormer. When Joe Grant got to Saudi Arabia, there were only two airfields, one at Dhahran and the other at Jeddah, both improved as a military necessity. King Abdulaziz had a landing strip at Taif, where he had his summer palace. If the King wanted his airplane somewhere else, Joe had to pick out a likely spot to put the DC-3 down from the air. There were no landmarks, no large cities, and no one to talk to on the radio. Joe pretty much depended on the Saudis to find the places where the King wanted his plane. When he got there, he took a fix on the stars to find out where he was.

KING ABDULAZIZ, HIS PLANE AND HIS PILOT

Many of these early images are from slides Joe Grant had taken of the Royal DC-3's and the Saudi Arabian Airline aircraft, a few are in color.

In 2006, Joe Grant returned to Saudi Arabia as a guest of the royal family. As he toured the places he'd seen 60 years before, he saw the development as the natural evolution of the vision of the man he knew—King Abdulaziz. "He was one of the greatest men of our time. He wanted to bring his people up to what this great country is now. What a transformation!"

*(**Left**) Joe, at the age of 100, not ready to retire he goes to work everyday making puzzle rings near his home in Stamford, Conneticut USA.*

*(**Lower Left**) Joe and his wife Marga.*

*(**Below**) HRH Prince Sultan bin Salman and Joe Grant share stories of their flying adventures.*

Promise of Oil

When the Kingdom of Saudi Arabia signed a concession agreement with Standard Oil of California (Socal) to explore for oil in the peninsula of Arabia in 1933, the concession covered some 320,000 square miles of desert, largely unsullied by any kind of road. Within months of signing, the oil company that turned into the Arabian American Oil Company, known to all as Aramco, had ordered its first airplane to serve as an aerial "eye" to the geological formations which held the promise of immense wealth—the promise of oil.

Just as aviation had changed the way that King Abdulaziz could move around his kingdom, aviation compressed time for Aramco. Exploring the vast concession by conventional means—trucks and four-wheel-drive cars—would have taken months and years. And when it came to the tasks of supplying the drilling rigs, manning and maintaining camps and pumping stations, and patrolling the pipeline, aircraft were (and remain) the only answer. The idea of running trucks and cars in and out of these remote areas (where it's feasible at all) would be prohibitively time consuming and expensive. By 1948, Aramco had an Aviation Department and was operating a kind of domestic fleet of airplanes for both exploration and to shuttle people and equipment within the Kingdom (and an occasional foray to Beirut or Baghdad)—eight DC-3s and five Navions. In 1955 Aramco replaced most of the Navions with DHC-2 Beavers. Each airplane had a particular use.

Aramco airplane overflying an early oil well in Saudi Arabia. This photograph and the ones on the following pages were provided by Aramco.

Aramco's Beavers were the airplanes that went into the really remote places. The planes need only short distances for take-off, have good range and speed, and were used to haul passengers and cargo from the main exploration camps to the small temporary camps of the "oil hunters." The Beavers were the small trucks of the fleet, carrying 1,200 to 1,500 pounds of passengers, water, food, and fuel, and were flying an average of thirty hours a week.

KING ABDULAZIZ, HIS PLANE AND HIS PILOT

Just as it was for most airlines of the period, the DC-3 was the mainstay of the Aramco fleet. The first DC-3 (a converted C-47) came on board in 1947, and the last was retired in 1976—a clear indication of the value of the aircraft. The primary use over the span of years was what came to be called the "Milk Run"—a flight along the 1,068 mile-long crude oil pipeline from Dhahran to Beirut and the pumping stations in between. The passengers were oil company employees and their families; cargo could be anything, "from machinery, drilling or pumphouse equipment, parts…fresh and frozen foods, refrigerators, radios, Christmas trees…" The DC-3 was used for larger cargo than the Beavers could carry, "food, drummed water, drummed aviation gasoline for the Beavers, and general supplies." Just as Joe Grant did, Aramco pilots landed the DC-3s on "runways" marked out with tire tracks, oil drums and flares.

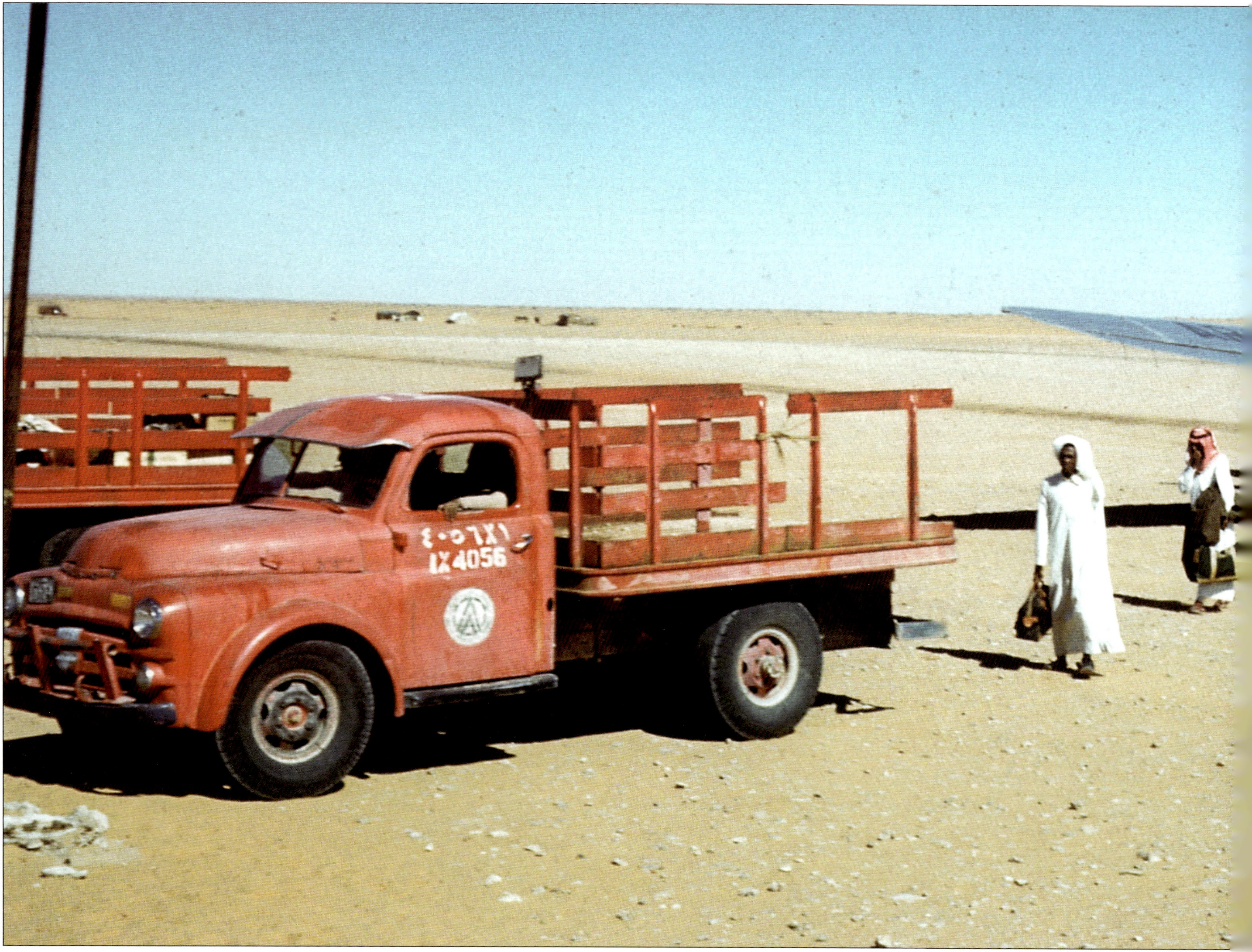
IX4056

49

KING ABDULAZIZ, HIS PLANE AND HIS PILOT

Even as early as 1948, most of the maintenance of the aircraft was done in Dhahran. The nearest Douglas overhaul base was at Bangalore, India. The safety record of the DC-3 with Aramco is nearly perfect—only one aircraft went down in a forced landing in a sandstorm. The plane landed wheels-up; no one was injured, and, "Sun and Flare," (the Aramco newsletter), reported that "damage was slight, and after repairs are completed it will be flown to Dhahran."

KING ABDULAZIZ, HIS PLANE AND HIS PILOT

53

KING ABDULAZIZ, HIS PLANE AND HIS PILOT

Before Aramco acquired the Beavers, Navions were the desert-based aircraft used for light cargo and personnel. "One of their interesting jobs is pipeline patrol. Skimming over a line at 120 miles an hour, a pilot can easily spot a leak, for the dark-colored oil stains the sand. Two-way radio linkage between the plane and maintenance cars means a crew can be guided to the break in a hurry."

When Saudi Arabian Airlines was started in 1946, the vision for the airline was two-fold: to ferry people, mail, and cargo within the Kingdom, and to enable Muslims to make the pilgrimage to Makkah. The fledgling airline was limited by the range and size of its DC-3s. The earliest routes connected Riyadh with Jeddah, Madinah, Taif, Dhahran, and Hofuf. Jeddah was linked to Cairo, and, in 1948, to Damascus and Beirut. Transatlantic service to and from the Kingdom in 1946 was limited to TWA passenger service through Dhahran. In the 1950s Saudi Arabian Airlines expanded its passenger fleet, adding 10 Convair 340s and two DC-4s. The expansion was in large part a response to the growing demand from Muslim pilgrims wanting to travel to Makkah and Madinah, and the airline's destinations—Kuwait, Jordan, Pakistan, Istanbul among them—reflected that demand.

KING ABDULAZIZ, HIS PLANE AND HIS PILOT

The rapid development of the oilfields and the need to bring people and equipment to the Kingdom was beyond the capacity of Saudi Arabian Airlines and TWA. In 1947 Aramco inaugurated its own transatlantic passenger service with the "Flying Camel"—a DC-4—flying from New York to Dhahran, with stops in the Azores, Lisbon, Rome, and Beirut. A second DC-4, dubbed the "Flying Gazelle," was brought on later the same year. It wasn't until 1961 that commercial aviation made the Aramco's own transatlantic flights (by then DC-6s) redundant.

57

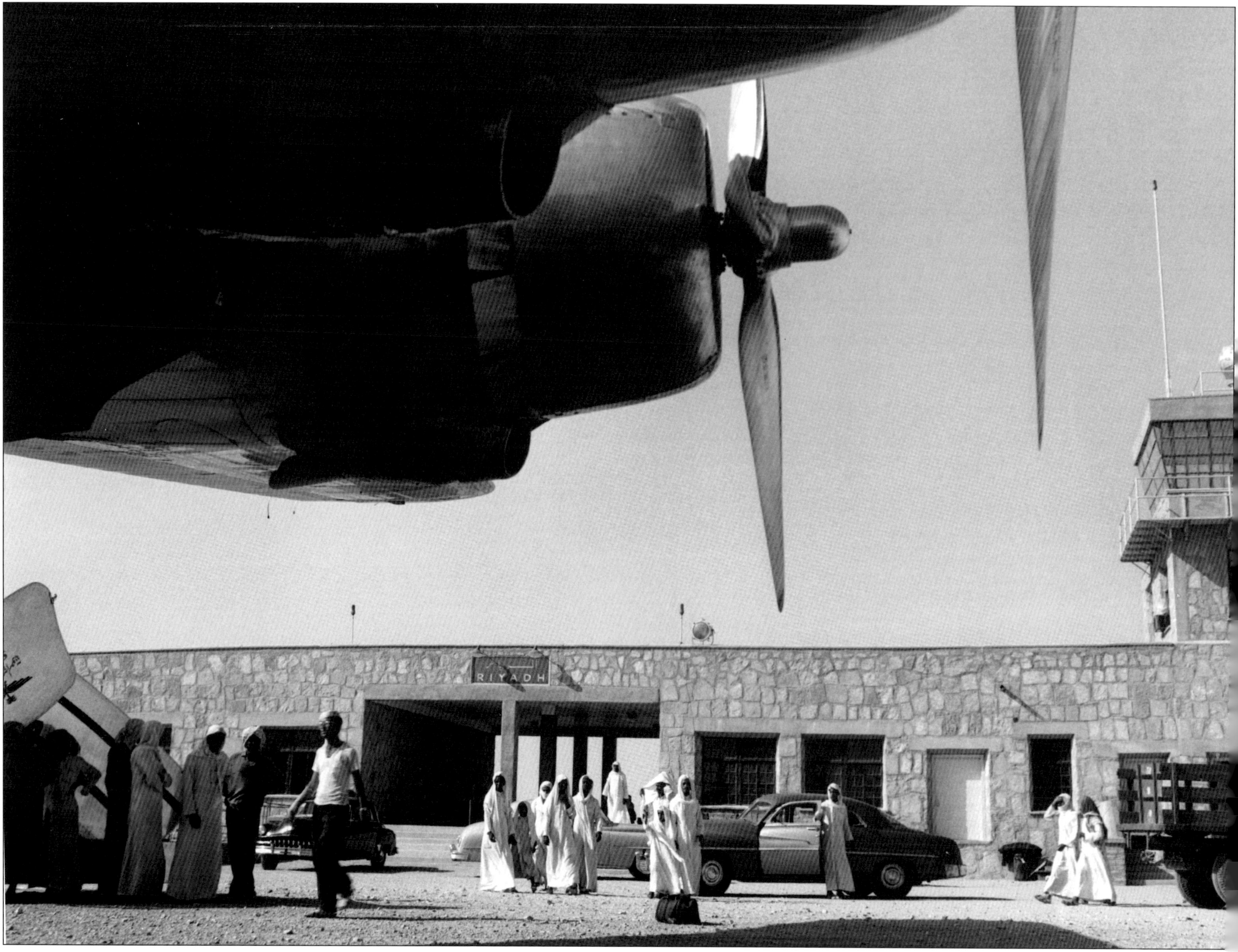
RIYADH

In 1946 the only "airports" in Saudi Arabia were at Jeddah and Dhahran. The field at Jeddah had been in use for some time, even prior to the unification of the Kingdom. The Dhahran airfield was built by the American military, under a 1945 agreement. As additional routes were established, airstrips were located by where pilots chose to land, and passenger services as we know them today—making reservations, tickets and so on, were rudimentary.

Saudi Arabian Airlines DC-3 preparing to take-off from airport.

KING ABDULAZIZ, HIS PLANE AND HIS PILOT

Considering the volume of air traffic that was taking place in the Kingdom in those early years, and considering the lack of developed facilities and the harshness of the conditions, the safety record of civil aviation in the Kingdom in those years was remarkable. One of two forced landings was on January 2, 1953. A DC-4 operated by KLM en route from London to Karachi ran into fog at its scheduled stop at Basra, in Iraq. All the nearby alternatives were closed by the same weather, so the pilot tried to make it to Dhahran. The airplane ran out of fuel "with its goal in sight," and was forced down in the dunes about four miles south of Qatif.

King Abdulaziz, his plane and his pilot

Flying in the sand and heat of the desert makes maintenance even more a part of the aviation scene than ever. Early on, major repairs and overhauls had to be performed outside Saudi Arabia, but routine maintenance, for both Saudi Arabian Airlines and Aramco, was done in-house—in the case of Joe Grant and the original crews of Saudi Arabian Airlines, by the pilots themselves.

Aramco quickly built up its maintenance operation. By the 1960s, Aramco was doing almost all its own maintenance and repair in Dhahran—"everything from propellers and brakes to radios and seat cushions."

KING ABDULAZIZ, HIS PLANE AND HIS PILOT

Evolution of Saudi Arabian Airlines logos

65

T-6 Saudi Trainers

67

In 1949, Saudi Arabian Airlines bought five Bristol 170 freighters to diversify the fleet. These aircraft could be adapted for cargo or passenger use—the seats could be removed easily—and could be loaded through clamshell doors at the front. The aircraft remained in service until 1958.

(Below) According to an illustrated history of the airline, Saudi Arabian Airlines bought four of these Lockheed Lodestars in 1950. Only one may have been delivered to the Kingdom, but was never put into service.

KING ABDULAZIZ, HIS PLANE AND HIS PILOT

There were a number of years in which airlines operated without the luxury of buildings. Nevertheless, the protocols of immigration were maintained—passports and visas still had to be stamped. The SAA emblem on the front of the aircraft indicates that the photo was taken prior to 1952, when the airline's abbreviation was changed to SDI to avoid duplication with South African Airways.

With the Royal DC-3s (SA-R-1, 2, and 3) and the next generation airliner, the DC-4 (SA-R-4), Saudi Arabia took a larger diplomatic role in regional and world affairs. Prince, and later, King Faisal had been Saudi Arabia's diplomatic face since he was 14 years old (in 1919, he represented his father, King Abdulaziz on a diplomatic mission to England, and since 1926 he had been the Kingdom's de facto foreign minister), but the speed and convenience of air travel allowed him to travel quickly to give Saudi Arabia a voice in changing regional affairs. Crown Prince (and in 1953, King) Saud used the aircraft on state visits to regional powers such as Egypt and Lebanon, and the airfields at Jeddah and Riyadh allowed state visits to the Kingdom from regional and international powers.

KING ABDULAZIZ, HIS PLANE AND HIS PILOT

(Below)
King Saud with King Hussein of Jordan, and Prince Nawaf in Dhahran in 1953

(Above)
Crown Prince (later King) Faisal arriving on an official visit

Artifacts

When Joe Grant and the other pilots and copilots were flying the first scheduled flights for Saudi Arabian Airlines, they didn't think of themselves as making history. Joe says he was just doing a job, working for the King. As a result, few if any records of the day-to-day operations of the fledgling airline—flight schedules, tickets, and the like—exist today.

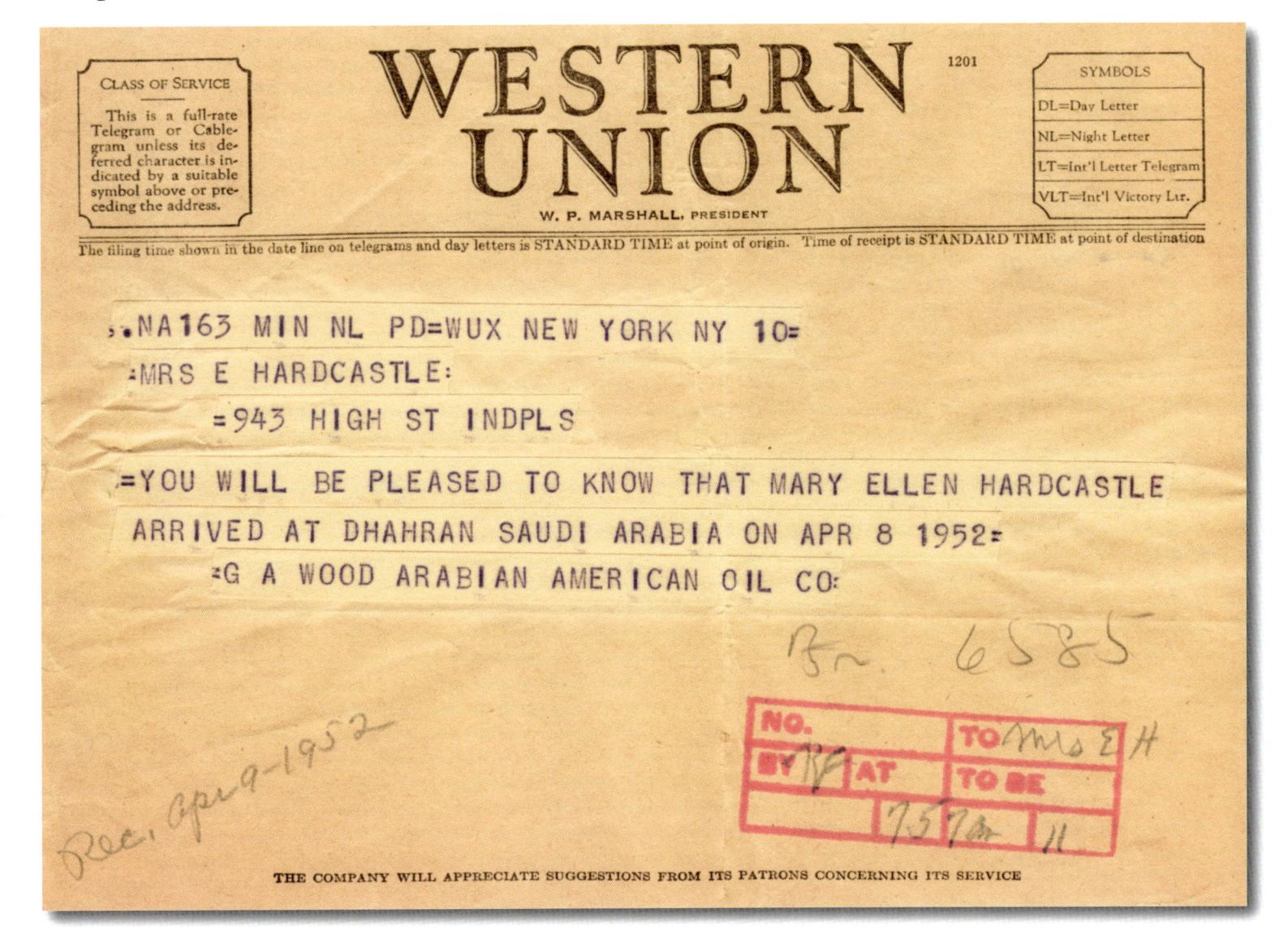

WESTERN UNION

W. P. MARSHALL, PRESIDENT

CLASS OF SERVICE
This is a full-rate Telegram or Cablegram unless its deferred character is indicated by a suitable symbol above or preceding the address.

SYMBOLS
DL=Day Letter
NL=Night Letter
LT=Int'l Letter Telegram
VLT=Int'l Victory Ltr.

NA163 MIN NL PD=WUX NEW YORK NY 10=

MRS E HARDCASTLE=

=943 HIGH ST INDPLS

=YOU WILL BE PLEASED TO KNOW THAT MARY ELLEN HARDCASTLE ARRIVED AT DHAHRAN SAUDI ARABIA ON APR 8 1952=

=G A WOOD ARABIAN AMERICAN OIL CO=

KING ABDULAZIZ, HIS PLANE AND HIS PILOT

(Left)
Airline ticket receipt for TWA leaving Geneva arriving Dhahran 1954.

DC-6B
FLIGHT SCHEDULE

EASTBOUND	STATUTE MILES	DATE	LCT (Summer)	GMT	REMARKS
Lv-New York		Fri. Nov. 29	3:00 p.m.	2000	Dinner aboard
Ar-Gander	1140	Fri. Nov. 29	8:45 p.m.	0015	
Lv-Gander		Fri. Nov. 29	9:45 p.m.	0115	Breakfast aboard
Ar-Amsterdam	2590	Sat. Nov. 30	11:00 a.m.	1000	

OVERNIGHT IN AMSTERDAM (Bus lvs. hotel 1 hr. and 15 min. before plane departs.)

Lv-Amsterdam		Sun. Dec. 1	2:00 p.m.	1300	Lunch aboard
Ar-Rome	930	Sun. Dec. 1	6:00 p.m.	1700	Dinner on ground
Lv-Rome		Sun. Dec. 1	7:00 p.m.	1800	
Ar-Beirut	1425	Mon. Dec. 2	1:45 a.m.	2345	Breakfast on ground
Lv-Beirut		Mon. Dec. 2	2:45 a.m.	0045	Snack Service
Ar-Dhahran	1030	Mon. Dec. 2	9:00 a.m.	0500	

WESTBOUND

Lv-Dhahran		Tue. Dec. 3	8:30 a.m.	0430	Snack aboard
Ar-Beirut	1030	Tue. Dec. 3	10:00 a.m.	0900	
Lv-Beirut		Tue. Dec. 3	12:00 noon	1000	Lunch aboard
Ar-Rome	1425	Tue. Dec. 3	4:45 p.m.	1545	Dinner on ground
Lv-Rome		Tue. Dec. 3	5:45 p.m.	1645	Snack Service
Ar-Amsterdam	930	Tue. Dec. 3	9:30 p.m.	2030	

OVERNIGHT IN AMSTERDAM (Bus lvs. hotel 1 hr. and 15 min. before plane departs.)

Lv-Amsterdam		Wed. Dec. 4	6:30 p.m.	1730	
Ar-Shannon	640	Wed. Dec. 4	8:45 p.m.	2045	Dinner on ground
Lv-Shannon		Wed. Dec. 4	9:45 p.m.	2145	Breakfast aboard
Ar-New York	3120	Thu. Dec. 5	6:30 a.m.	1130	

ARABIAN AMERICAN OIL COMPANY

PASSENGER INFORMATION

FLIGHT NO: **G-178**   AIRCRAFT NO. **N-709-A**   NAME: **THE GAZELLE**

THE CREW

CAPTAIN: **CHARLES FISHER**

FIRST OFFICER: **ARCH McKELLAR**

FLIGHT ENGINEER: **JAMES TITCOMB**

NAVIGATOR: **PAUL HAMILTON**

RADIO OPERATOR: **FRED GUSSMAN**

PURSER: **HARRY WELSH**

STEWARDESS: **MARTHA MITROKA**

CHECK PILOT: _____

OTHER: _____

King Abdulaziz, his plane and his pilot

(Left)
Aramco flight schedule for the DC-6B, front and back.

Thanks to individuals who saved them as memorabilia, there are some records from the days when Aramco flew its employees internationally and within Saudi Arabia. The artifacts of that early history displayed on these pages are thanks to the generosity of former Aramco employees and family members. At first, Aramco flew DC-4s between New York and Dhahran, and touted the fact that they made the trip in less than thirty hours flying time. By 1954 the company was flying DC-6Bs. The usual New York to Dhahran routing was New York, Gander, Amsterdam, Rome, Beirut, Dhahran. The Gander to Amsterdam leg was some eleven hours in the air.

(Right)
Page 1 of the Passenger Information Booklet for Aramco Aircraft

ARABIAN AMERICAN OIL COMPANY
AVIATION DEPARTMENT

PASSENGER INFORMATION

AIRCRAFT RULES
1. The Captain is in complete charge while en route.
2. Observe the "Fasten Seat Belt" sign and "No Smoking" sign. Smoking is not allowed in the lavatories, in the berths, or in the aircraft or vicinity of the aircraft while on the ground.
3. Entrance to the crew compartment is permissible only with the approval of the Captain.
4. Cabin attendants are responsible for the cleanliness of the cabin and compartments and lavatories. Please do not make this part of their job difficult.
5. There are life preservers, life rafts and other special gear aboard for any emergency. The crew will give a short briefing on this subject.
6. Remain seated after landing until cleared to deplane.

COMMUNICATIONS
1. It is unlawful to carry any mail for delivery between different countries except that which is written in flight.
2. Commercial radio - telegraph service from the aircraft to any point in the U. S. is available at the rate of 18 cents per word.

YOUR LUGGAGE
1. Hand luggage and other articles may not be left on the airplane at overnight stops. Unchecked baggage and other personal articles are the complete responsibility of the passenger. Make sure all such items are on the bus with you before leaving the airport or the hotel.
2. Heavy checked luggage is stored in the hold of the plane and is available only at final destination. It is not available in flight or at enroute stations.

FOR YOUR COMFORT
1. There are magazines, stationery, playing cards, Astringosol, combs, razors, aspirin, sewing kits and other articles for passengers' convenience aboard the aircraft.
2. Additional sandwiches, pastries and fruit are available and will be served upon request.
3. The cabin attendants will be glad to answer any questions pertaining to the aircraft, route flown, points of interest, questions on Customs, Immigration, etc.
4. Passengers subject to air-sickness, or feeling the approach of air-sickness, should ask the cabin attendants for Bonamine. Paper containers for air-sickness are in the pockets of the chairs in the main cabin and in special pockets below left hand windows in the compartments.

MEALS
1. The meals during the short refueling stops are served in the airport restaurants and are paid for by Aramco through Trans-World Airlines or through K.L.M.
2. Any drinks ordered by the individual are for the individual's personal account and should be paid for when served.

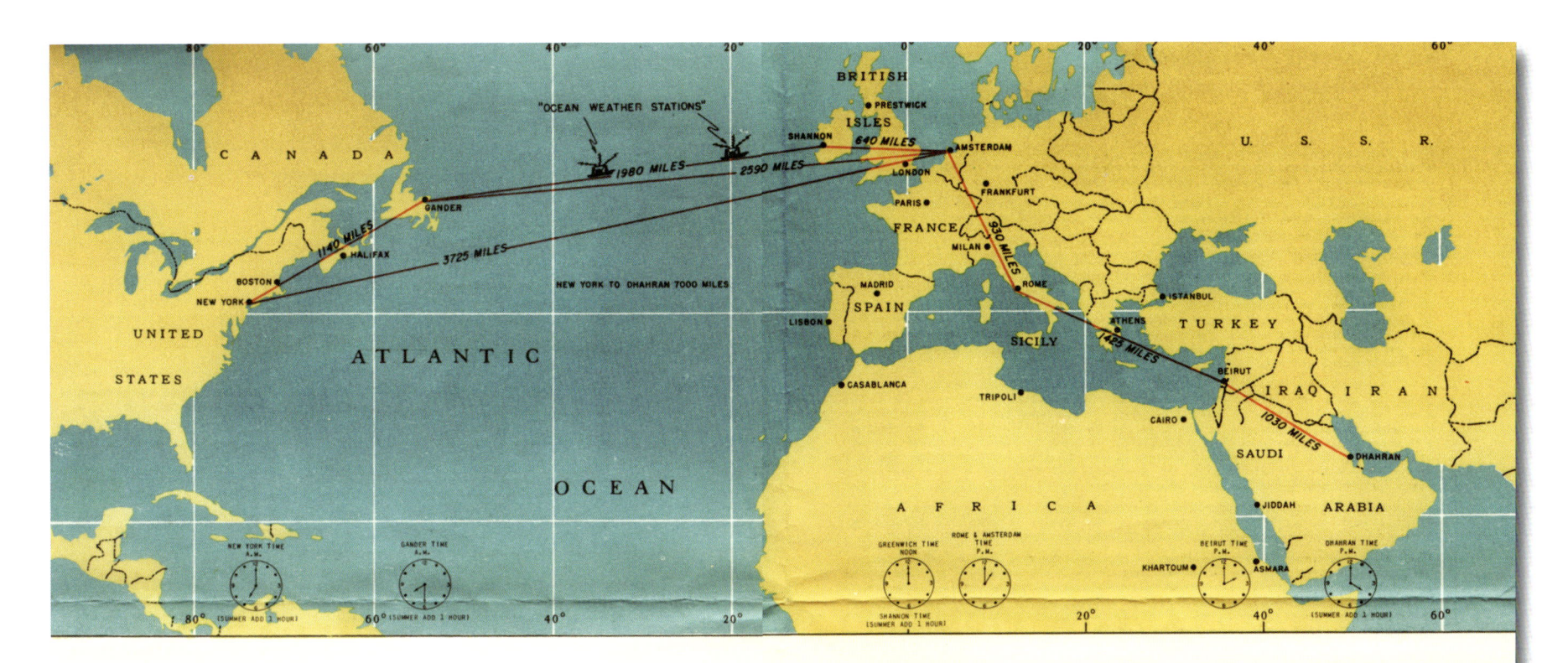

OVERNIGHT STOPS

1. Passports and immunization records must be carried on your person to be available on request.
2. At overnight stops, the KLM agent arranges for hotel reservations and transportation to and from the hotel. The transportation is paid by KLM for the Aramco account; hotel bills and meals must be paid by you. Your reservations will be in first-class hotels, and it is customary in Europe for men to wear business suits and neckties in the lobby, dining room, etc.
3. Hotels abroad do not provide free soap.
4. At overnight stops, the bus departs from the hotel 1 hour and 15 minutes before the plane's take-off time, and all passengers must be at the hotel ready for departure on time.

SOME FACTS ABOUT OUR PLANES

1. The slight change in the sound of the engines which you may hear every few hours is a result of the crew shifting the supercharger gears, so that proper oil circulation will be maintained around the clutches. The chattering sound you hear during taxiing, after take-off and before landing is caused by the pressure regulator of the hydraulic system.
2. "The Flying Camel" (N-708-A), "The Flying Gazelle" (N-709-A) and "The Flying Oryx" (N-710-A) are DC-6B's, manufactured by the Douglas Aircraft Company, Inc., Santa Monica, California. Their wing span is 117' and their length is 106'. Their maximum gross take-off weight is 107,000 lbs. and their average empty weight is 66,000 lbs. Their long-range cruising speed is approximately 285 MPH; however, their maximum level flight speed is 365 MPH. The total fuel capacity of each is 5,500 gallons. The passenger capacity of The Camel and The Gazelle is 46 persons when set up as a day plane, or 40 persons when the berths are utilized. The Flying Oryx' passenger capacity is normally 32 when berths are utilized; however, 38 may be carried when it is utilized as a day plane. In addition to these passengers, The Flying Oryx is also capable of carrying a maximum of 9,900 lbs. of large-size cargo in a specially equipped forward compartment.
3. The engines are R2800-CB17's, manufactured by Pratt & Whitney at East Hartford, Connecticut. Each develops 2,500 HP at take-off, with water/alcohol injection and 108/135 octane fuel. The long-range cruising power is approximately 1,100 HP per engine, at which rating the total fuel consumption is approximately 350 gallons per hour.
4. The cabins of all three aircraft are supercharged for your comfort, and the cabin pressure can be maintained at sea level up to a cruising altitude of 12,000'. At a cruising altitude of 20,000' the cabin pressure would be the equivalent of that of 5,000'. Although the cabin windows and doors are of more than adequate strength, they are not tamper proof. Since the pressure of the fuselage at times may be as high as 786 pounds per square foot, it is imperative that no one disturb the handles of the doors or emergency exits in flight. Particular care must also be taken to avoid scratching, striking or leaning against the plexiglass window panels.

CURRENCY EXCHANGE

1. In Amsterdam, Netherlands, the legal tender is the guilder. One U. S. Dollar equals approximately 3.75 guilders. In most countries of Europe the purchasing value of the dollar is slightly above the dollar value at home.

ARRIVING AT DHAHRAN

1. Newcomers to Dhahran should deplane last.

Passenger Information Booklet for Aramco Aircraft.

KING ABDULAZIZ, HIS PLANE AND HIS PILOT

Most of the photographs that record the history of civil aviation in Saudi Arabia were either black and white originally; or black and white copies of color originals are all that remain. Scattered throughout this book are rare color images that have been saved.

(Below) is one of Aramco's Convairs that flew between Middle Eastern cities and occasionally to Europe in the 1950s.

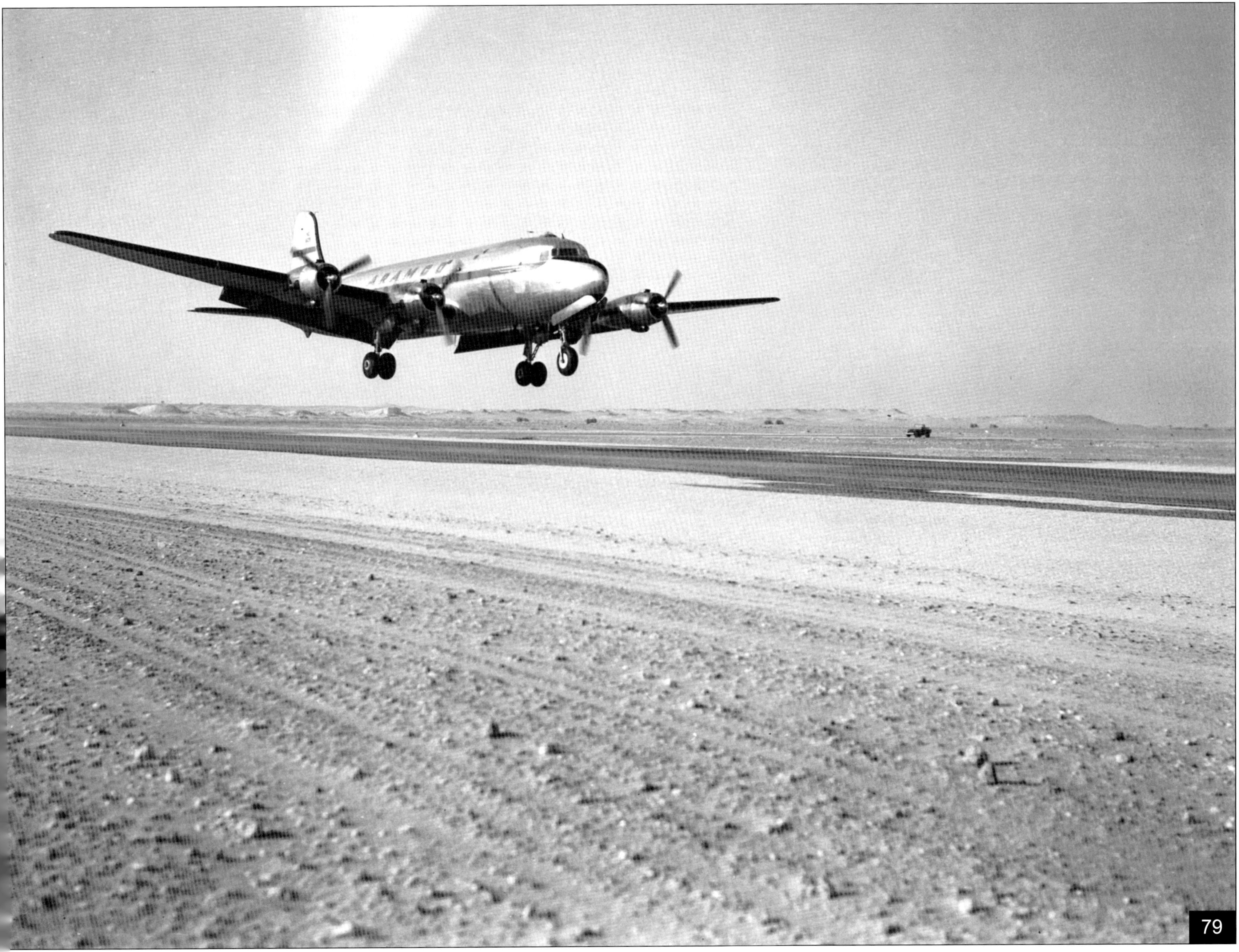
ARAMCO

KING ABDULAZIZ, HIS PLANE AND HIS PILOT

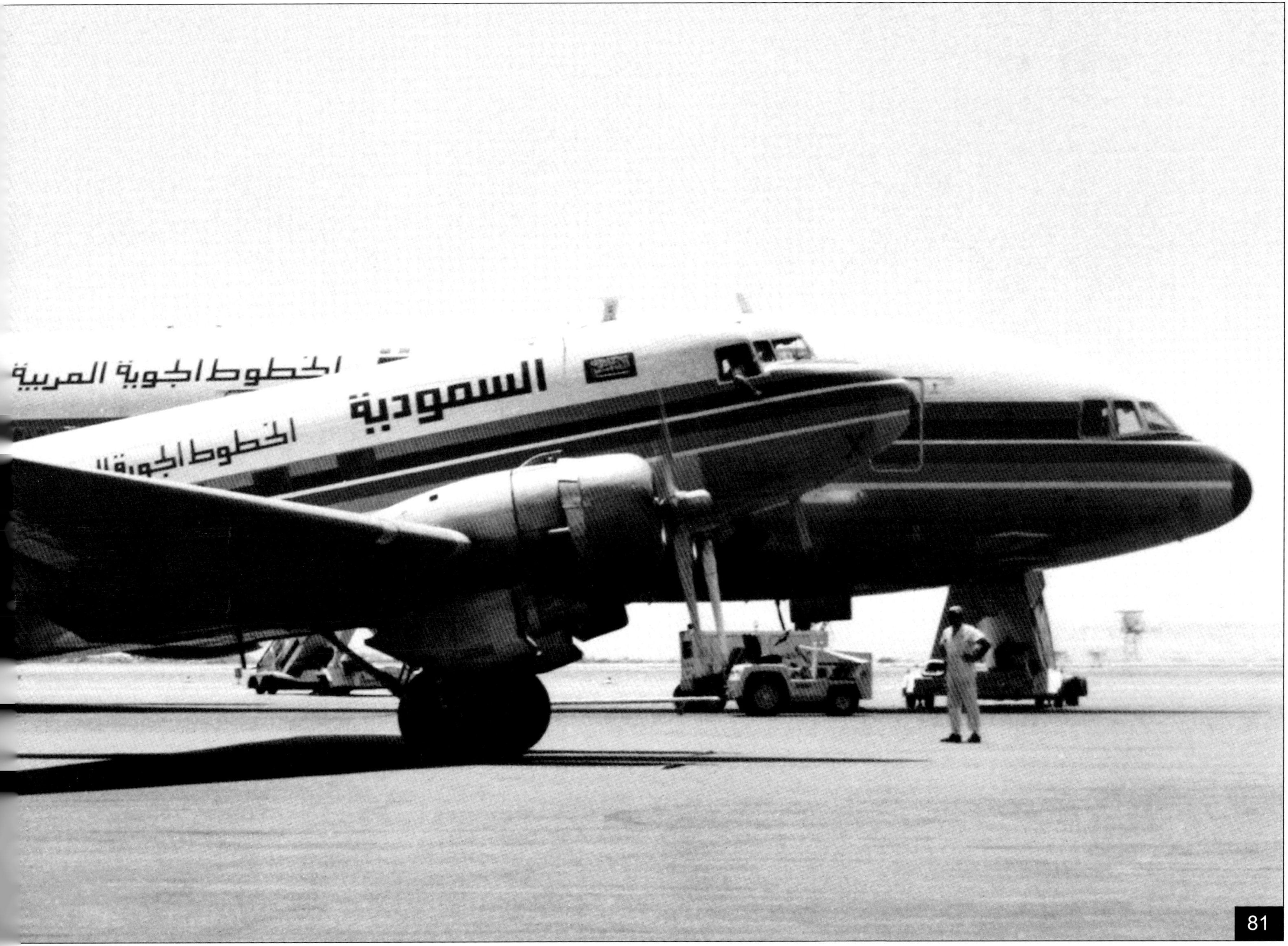
الخطوط الجوية العربية
السعودية
الخطوط الجوية

King Abdulaziz, his plane and his pilot

83

Restoration

The original gift DC-3 airplane served the King and the Kingdom for a long time, first as the King's personal airplane, SA-R-1. It's recorded that King Abdulaziz first flew in the airplane on September 30, 1945, from Afif to Taif. Later the DC-3 became one of the airliners in the growing fleet of DC-3s. It held various subsequent registrations: SA-T-1, and finally HZ-AAX.

The DC-3 served the Kingdom until 1977, a 32-year span, clocking some 32,000 hours. For 10 years following its retirement, the airplane sat out on the runway, neglected. In 1987 it was decided that the airplane should be turned into a static display, and it underwent the first of two restorations and was stored at Riyadh Air Force base.

In 1999, for the centennial of the Kingdom of Saudi Arabia, another restoration was undertaken by the Boeing Corporation, this time to return SA-R-1 to flying condition. The photographs on these pages are the various stages in the process, from disassembly and transport, to running up the engines prior to the first flight. The restoration was contracted to Royal Aviation; the work was done in Saudi Arabia.

The airplane now takes pride of place in the Saqr Al Jazeerah Air Museum in Riyadh, where people can go to see, and even sit in this great piece of Saudi Arabian aviation history.

(Above)
A few parts for the restoration of the DC-3 were obtained from an airframe resting in an aircraft junkyard outside of Riyadh.

(Right)
The aircraft in various stages of paint application. Photographs Courtesy of Boeing and Royal Aviation.

King Abdulaziz, his plane and his pilot

87

(At Right and Below) 1999 images of the restored DC3.

SA-R-1 as it sits today in the Saqr Al Jazeerah Air Museum in Riyadh. The original crossed swords emblem on the front of the door has been replaced by a centennial commemorative design.

KING ABDULAZIZ, HIS PLANE AND HIS PILOT

(Right) The engine cowlings are not the original cowlings that were on the King's DC-3, but a later addition to increase speed.

(Below) Seating capacity today is two rows of 14 seats; the seats can be stowed to increase available cargo space. There is a galley behind the cockpit doors and lavatory facilities in the rear.

KING ABDULAZIZ, HIS PLANE AND HIS PILOT

*(**Right and Below**) Joe Grant, back in the cockpit of the DC-3 after 60 years!*

SA-R-1

The Saqr Al Jazeerah Air Museum in Riyadh houses many examples of fixed wing aircraft and helicopters used by the Royal Saudi Air Force through its history.

An impressive collection of well maintained aircraft and artifacts are displayed throughout the museum.

From the front, the air museum reminds us of the undulating sand dunes all around.

Many larger aircraft are on display outside the museum.

(Left) C-130

(Below) T-33, Lightning and Tornado

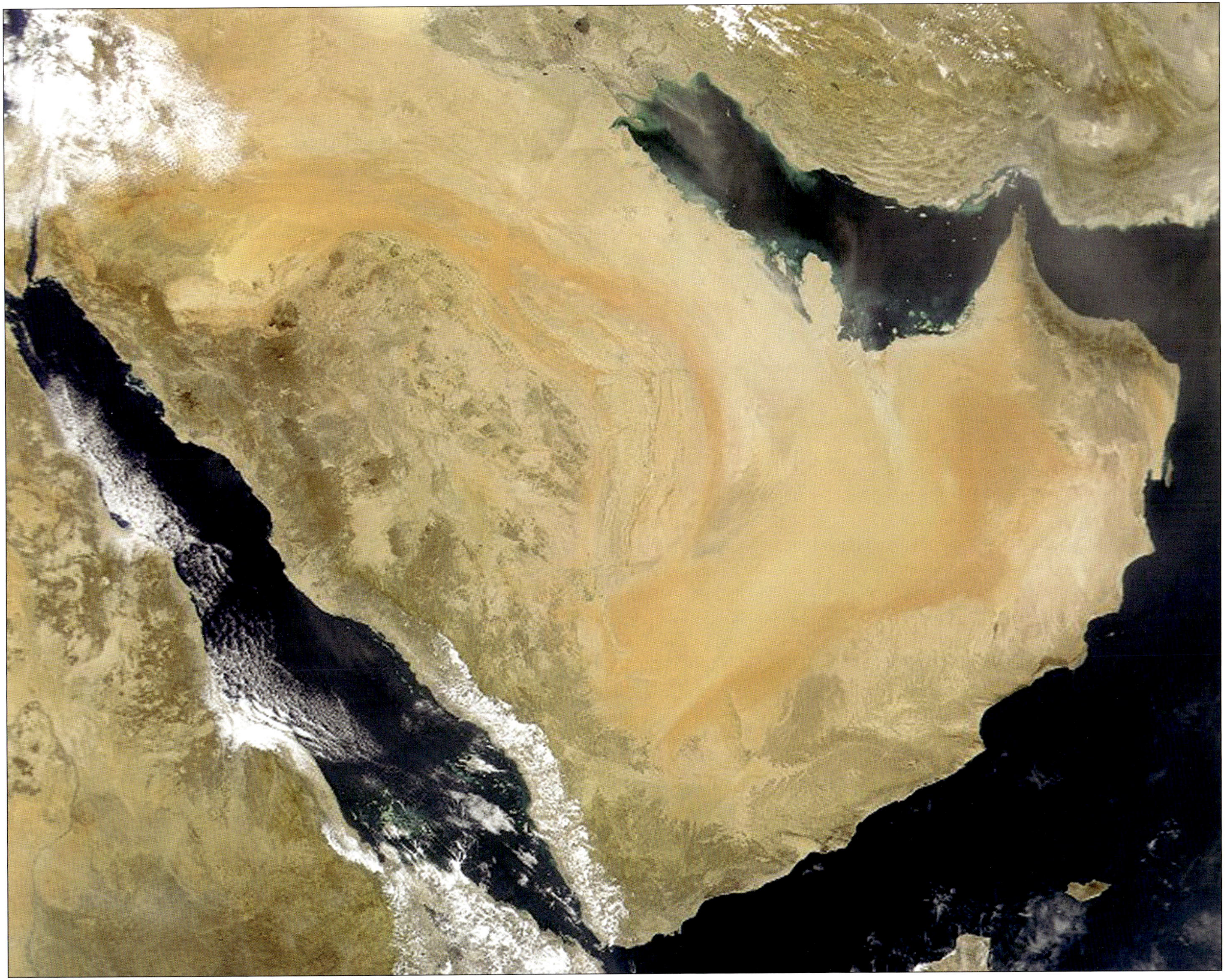

There is a new generation of flyers now in Saudi Arabia, which includes men such as Prince Sultan bin Salman, who are exploring new relationships between aviation and the development of the Kingdom. In 1985, Prince Sultan bin Salman became the first Saudi, first Arab and first Muslim to go into space as a member of the crew of the space shuttle Discovery. After returning to Earth, stepping off the airplane in Taif in his NASA flight suit, he realized that Saudi Arabia was "about to shift gears and go into a new era." It recalls the time when the DC-3 helped his grandfather, King Abdulaziz, step into the modern world. From now on, Saudi Arabia would look different.

HRH Prince Sultan bin Salmon aboard the space shuttle discovery, June 1985. Photograph courtesy NASA.

During the first orbit, the astronauts all looked for their own countries; later, they began to see their countries in the contexts of regions, and continents. And finally, they saw themselves as part of the world as a whole—a completely new context.

These days, Prince Sultan and others in the Saudi Aviation Club want to see their country new ways—flying, to be sure, but in a different way. For Prince Sultan it may be because he saw the country from space, that now he wants to see it in detail, desert and mountains, flying low level, in a glider or in high altitude jets. It may be that this kind of aviation will become part of the future of the Kingdom, as the country gains a reputation as a premier place to soar.

The Kingdom of Saudi Arabia has modernized at an extraordinary pace. The benefits are apparent to everyone—large modern cities, highways, beautiful airports and architecture. At the same time, daily life in the Kingdom is distinctly Saudi, in manner, in dress, in custom. Just as it was for King Abdulaziz, the concern for leaders of the country is to sustain that unique heritage in the face of an increasingly global sense of the world.

One part of the vision that King Abdulaziz had for aviation was that ease of movement throughout the Kingdom would give the far regions of the country a sense that they were one nation. That vision persists today. Many of the country's leading citizens have expressed concern that the nation find a balance that does not diminish the values of tradition and heritage.

(Left) HRH Prince Sultan bin Salmon glides above the desert.

(Right) HRH Prince Sultan bin Salmon Prepares to pilot the F-15.

KING ABDULAZIZ, HIS PLANE AND HIS PILOT

June, 2009 Visit

In June of 2009, Captain Joe Grant, now 101 years old, returned to Saudi Arabia. Earlier in the year, Joe was awarded the King Abdulaziz Medal First Class on behalf of King Abdullah bin Abdulaziz by Saudi Arabian Ambassador to the United States, Adel Al Jubeir. The King Abdulaziz Medal First Class is the highest civilian medal awarded by Saudi Arabia and is awarded in recognition of significant contributions made by an individual to the Kingdom.

Joe shares a story with HRH Prince Bandar bin Abdulaziz

Captain Grant was invited to Saudi Arabia to meet King Abdullah and other senior members of the royal family who have been his friends and were frequent passengers in the mid 1940's as young men and children. The highlight of his trip was a personal audience with King Abdullah. The King greeted all of us with a lavish celebration at his farm in Janadriyah. The King and Joe had not seen each other in over sixty years. When the King first saw Joe, he said, "Joseph, your face is still the same."

Joe and the King, in the presence of other senior royal family members and other important Saudi personalities spent over three hours together. Joe was amazed with all the recognition from everyone, particularly his former passengers, who were all young

HRH Prince Bader bin Abdulaziz and Joe discuss a photograph.

men and boys when he transported them across desert sands. They reminded him of the trials and tribulations of flying in Saudi Arabia in those early days of aviation.

They also recalled numerous incidents involving Joe and his fine flying skills. One incident recalled was when Captain Grant picked up a lady passenger from an outlaying area of Saudi Arabia. She was to be transported back to Riyadh to receive immediate medical care. As Joe was preparing to land, he tried to put down the landing gear, but only one wheel came down. Nothing worked when he tried to activate the other wheel.

(Upper Right) Joe Grant and HRH Prince Naif bin Abdulaziz.

(Right) Joe Grant and HRH Prince Salman bin Abdulaziz.

(Below) HRH Prince Muqrin bin Abdulaziz reminisces with Captain Joe.

Joe, in turn, had to try an emergency landing procedure whereby he would come down and bounce the one wheel off the sand and hoped that the action would free the other wheel and send it down. IT WORKED... Joe then lifted the plane back into the air, made another pass and safely landed his beloved DC-3 with all the passengers intact.

Joe's comment when they retold this and other stories about how much they appreciated his service to Saudi Arabia was, "I was just doing my job."

Throughout this small history, we've shown how aviation was a significant tool in the modernization of the Kingdom of Saudi Arabia, beginning with King Abdulaziz and his DC-3. Other regional powers had a vast head start in terms of development—transportation, governmental institutions, and the economic structure of the country.

When development takes place—has to take place—at the rate it did in Saudi Arabia, there is no guidebook. There's no plan to follow, no model. Sometimes development begins to drive itself, as aviation did, when, with airplanes there was a sudden need for airports, maintenance, fueling stations, passenger service, immigration control structures, and, of course, trained people to man those tasks. King Abdulaziz and his sons have had to be guided largely by their own vision and instincts to take the Kingdom forward.

Other regional powers took their models from colonizing nations. Saudi Arabia has never been colonized, and so development has had a uniquely Saudi character. Amid the modern cities, highways, airports, and architecture, daily life in the Kingdom would still be recognized by King Abdulaziz as distinctly Saudi.

When Joe Grant returned to the Kingdom in 2006, after 60 years, he found the cities transformed, but Saudi traditions unchanged. "What a wonderful culture! I don't know whether the king awakened a culture that was already there, or if he just perfected a culture that existed…."

KING ABDULAZIZ, HIS PLANE AND HIS PILOT

Saudi Arabian Airlines today has grown into the largest airline in the region. The Kingdom operates three international airports (King Khalid International Airport in Riyadh, King Fahd International Airport in Damman, and King Abdul Aziz International Airport in Jeddah, still the busiest airport in the Kingdom). In addition there are four regional airports and 16 domestic airports.

"Today Saudi Arabian Airlines has some ninety one aircraft, including the latest and most advanced wide-bodied jets presently available, flies to more than ninety destinations worldwide, and … carried more than eighteen million passengers in 2007." From small beginnings, the Kingdom has come far.

Epilogue

Joe Grant, with Irene Hansen

Joe Grant reminisces about his time piloting the DC-3 presented by President Franklin D. Roosevelt to King Abdulaziz Al Saud of Saudi Arabia. Fifty years after his service as personal pilot to the royal family, Joe returned to Saudi Arabia. These are his reflections.

I spent two years in Saudi Arabia flying the DC-3 for the royal family, and when I got back to the United States, I would have walked back if I could have. Here in Saudi, I am amongst my friends. My time in Saudi Arabia was the greatest gift I could ever have been given. At the time, I didn't realize what an opportunity it was! I thought I was just doing my job.

From its beginning, Saudi Arabia has demonstrated more than any country what can be done when you are given the chance. It all goes back to one person, and that was King Abdulaziz. After fifty years, I went back to Saudi at age ninety-eight. I am so very grateful. I can still remember the King with his huge hands on my shoulder. And there was my old airplane, my baby-what a beautiful memory. There has been a tremendous change in aviation since my days in Saudi Arabia. I am so proud of what has been accomplished and my small role in its history.

When I was a boy, my Uncle Leigh Wade made an around-the-world flight attempt. My love of flying and aviation comes from him. I spent four years flying in the Army, and then spent many years barnstorming, ferrying and doing odd flying jobs. My brother Roy and I tried to make a living as stunt flyers. One of us would talk people into flying with us for $5.00; the other would take them up in the plane and try to scare them half to death with crazy stunts! My nickname was Crazy Pilot. I finally landed a job with TWA and the next thing I knew I was on my way to Cairo and to the Kingdom. There were three of us, including a radio operator named Zed Lockhart and another man named Mark Outhwaite. We had no idea of what we were there for!

We started out by flying the DC-3 to Jeddah. King Abdulaziz's son, Prince Faisal, and his entourage were with us on that first flight. It was an introduction to a world I didn't know. No words can adequately describe the people who gave me such wonderful memories. Their warmth and generosity lives in my heart. It is a gift that has stayed with me.

Zed, now named Abuzed, Mark and I first were stationed at the Palace in Riyadh. We were a spoiled bunch and complained at being confined in one area when there was so much going on at the Palace! We went back to a hotel in Jeddah and then finally built quarters at the airport. Except for an electric plant and trips to Cairo for parts, the airport was home.

In those early days there were only two airports in Saudi Arabia, and they were dirt strips in Dhahran and Jeddah. The DC-3 was luxury though! When President Roosevelt wanted to give an airplane to the King as a gift, he gave him the best we had to offer. The King loved to fly…there couldn't have been a better gift than that airplane.

We took hunting trips-a party would find a good spot and set up a tent city. A guide would fly with us, sitting behind us in the cockpit and pointing out the way. We would land in the sand. On the first run coming, we would just touch the wheels down to see if the sand would hold our weight. In the evening, we would get a four star fix to figure out where we were!

A good many of our destinations were small villages. This was the beginning of the domestic route that followed. We could land anywhere-it was like my barnstorming days! After finding a good landing spot, we would set rocks or whatever we could find to mark the runway. It doesn't rain a lot in Saudi Arabia, but we got caught in the mud after a storm once. It took three vehicles to pull the plane out!

When I first arrived I bought a book so that I could learn Arabic. I always had it in my pocket. The Bedouins would play a game that I never figured out, but I would sit and listen. It was during these times that I realized that these seemingly uneducated people had a name for every star and that they could find their way across the desert by the stars. They never got lost.

When the King wanted to fly, Colonel Tassan would tell us that his Majesty wanted the airplane and we would be ready to go when he arrived. When we arrived at our destination the guards would take over the airplane and we were off duty. The King always made sure that we had our own tent, and I was privileged to have dinner with him on a number of occasions.

Being with the King always gave me a special feeling. This man was one of the most unusual of our era. He could face anything and remain in command of the situation. You couldn't help but admire him. Not only was he a King in title, he was the peoples' King. He was genuinely interested in everyone, including us. He always asked about our children and our plans for our families. You could feel the warmth of his heart. It is the basic philosophies of this man that have made Saudi Arabia one of the greatest countries in the world. He is still in the hearts and minds of the people who are shaping Saudi Arabia. To this day, the King meets with ordinary people on Mondays. They speak with him, air their thoughts, complaints and concerns, and the King hosts them for dinner.

Abuzed was supposed to be the radio operator, but once we arrived all of our radio operators were Saudis. Abuzed did many other things, though, including maintenance on the planes. The co-pilots were also Saudi; there was Hamsa, Saudi, Metasak, and later Kamilhami. Hamsa was my favorite and I flew with him most of the time. He was an excellent pilot and intelligent man.

Prince Faisal (later King Faisal) played a major role in starting the Saudi Arabian Airlines. We bought more airplanes from the army in Cairo. We had been briefed by TWA that the airline dreamed of having a worldwide airline and I think they had a bit if an axe to grind when Saudi Arabia began buying its own planes and starting its own airline. There were dreams of flights to Cairo and Damascus, but then it was still a domestic line. We would head out to two or three little towns and pick up passengers and cargo. We just opened the doors and filled up the airplane!

My time with King Abdulaziz and with the people of Saudi Arabia was a highlight of my 100 years on this earth. I will treasure the memories forever; I am honored to have played just a small role in the beginning of the country and in the development of aviation in this magnificent land. We all have dreams-it is amazing to think of what I have been given. I am so grateful.

Postscript

Indomitable Men

Joe Grant walked into the majlis of HRH Prince Salman bin Abdulaziz. The prince rose from his chair. "Joseph, Joseph, do you remember me?" Joe answered, "Well, you look just like your father." "But do you remember me?" exclaimed the prince. "Well, you sound like your father, too", stated Joe. "Joseph", said the Prince recalling the first and only previous meeting with Joe over 60 years before. "I was 8 years old, I boarded your plane for the first time. I remember you in your uniform. You were so striking to me. You were the first American I had ever seen. And you were so nice to me and my family. Remember how you took us to that swimming hole and we all went swimming together?" Joe just gleamed as he and the Prince hugged warmly and shook hands over and over. "My goodness, was that you? It is so good to see you again."

HRH Prince Salman bin Abdulaziz and Joe Grant.

Joe Grant and HRH Prince Salman's father, the founder of the Kingdom of Saudi Arabia, HM King Abdulaziz Al Saud, were and are both great men. They created special bonds with one another. When Joe delivered the DC-3 to the King and landed in the desert near the royal palace in Riyadh, King Abdulaziz saw something special in Joe and in the plane that Joe piloted into the interior of Saudi Arabia. He saw the future of the people of Saudi Arabia coming closer together and becoming a modern nation through the miracle of flight and the guidance of a truly historical figure in the aviation history.

Joe Grant who began his aviation career as an aircraft mechanic and a pilot in post World War I bi-wing airplanes, was the right man at the right time to work with a King who had a vision for the future of the Kingdom. Joe was given quarters in the royal palace and stayed with the King for two years as his personal pilot and advisor. "We ferried the royal family wherever they wanted to go. It was a great adventure. We would put the DC-3 down anywhere in the desert. We would just find a hard spot and land there with him."

I have had the special privilege of meeting and becoming a friend of a great man, Joe Grant. And I have learned so much about another great man, King Abdulaziz of Saudi Arabia, through the eyes of Joe Grant. The wisdom of these two men is now part of the wisdom of the ages. Joe called me recently and said, "Michael I am starting a new business, we have to get moving on this. We don't have forever, you know."

About the Author

Michael Saba PhD

With over 30 years of experience in Middle East relations, Dr. Saba's passion for the Kingdom of Saudi Arabia is rooted in its people, culture and society. Saba is the former president of Saba and Associates, a company that facilitated joint ventures between health care institutions around the world, developed fund raising strategies to apply to foreign countries, and demonstrated cross cultural concerns in the U.S. and abroad. He was also the founder of GULFAMERICA, an international business services company that facilitated trade between the U.S. and the Arab Gulf. Formerly Manager of Middle East Public Affairs for Mobil Oil Corporation, Saba has been working internationally since the 1960's. Dr. Saba was the first CEO of National Association of Arab Americans and was also the first Executive Director of Friends of Saudi Arabia.

Photo Credits, Sources

Al Turath Foundation

King Abdulaziz Foundation

Boeing

Saudi Arabia Airlines

Aramco

Royal Aviation

Al Jazeerah Aviation Museum

Joe Grant's Personal Collection

NASA, Lyndon B. Johnson Space Center

Vision Video, Inc.

111